Contents

Preface

As a high school student, you are faced with many decisions: should I join choir, should I try out for the basketball team, what can I do to be accepted by other students and teachers? The list goes on and on. One of the biggest decisions you will face is what to do after you graduate from high school. Some parents strongly encourage their children to attend college right away to secure a successful career. However, you may not feel ready for college, and you want to explore another path.

As a young person, I attended college for a year and quickly realized I wasn't fully prepared for it. I wanted a different challenge. So, I joined the military, and it proved to be the best decision I ever made.

Joining the military provided me with opportunities I would not have otherwise had at that point in my life. I got to travel around the world, make lifelong friends from very different backgrounds, and received an invaluable overall experience. I learned how to be an effective leader, how to accomplish tasks in a timely manner, and many other positive skills that have been valuable in the civilian world.

The decision to join the military is not an easy one, nor is the military an easier path than attending college. Yet it can be a life-changing experience that can lead to future success in your life journey.

I decided to write this book to share my own experience in the military and how the military helped mold a confused and lost nineteen-year-old who was scared of failure and unsure what the future held into the more focused, determined, caring, and thankful person I am today.

I have raised a few teenagers myself, and I am aware that there are still many high school students today who are not interested in college and unsure—and possibly even afraid—of what their future looks like, much as I was thirty years ago. If you are unsure what you want to do after high school, I hope that reading about my journey will help you decide if the military is a good option for you at this time in your life.

"The only impossible journey is the one you never begin." - Tony Robbins

Chapter 1. The Early Years

I grew up in the Midwest and had a fairly normal childhood. My father worked full-time, and my mother worked part-time. My two brothers are ten and twelve years older than me, so I sort of grew up like an only child. I had several close friends, was involved with sports and school organizations, and worked part-time.

As high school students in the late 1980s, most of my classmates started thinking about college choices as sophomores and juniors. I, on the other hand, was more focused on enjoying whatever I was doing at any given moment. By the time I was a senior, I decided I wanted to play football in college. I had a few opportunities at some small colleges and chose a school that was two hours from my hometown. I was excited to leave the nest and be on my own for the first time.

So, off to college I went. I quickly became friends with several other freshman football players. They grew up in a nearby town and were as unfocused on school as I was. Instead of going to class and studying, we spent most of our time enjoying the nightlife.

By mid-semester, I realized I was not in a good place and was having a hard time concentrating on my purpose at this stage in life. I had gotten good grades in high school and could accomplish the same at college, but I had a more fixed mindset at that time, rather than a growth mindset. I couldn't focus on my studies or even on football. I felt lost and miserable. I decided to move back home after the semester ended and attend a junior college in my hometown.

However, after being home for a few weeks, I realized this was not the answer, either. I reconnected with some of my friends from high school and enjoyed hanging out with them, but I still wasn't focused on my studies.

I started thinking about what I might do instead of college since I was not ready or focused enough for college at that time in my life. I enjoyed growing up in the community I did, but I was confident that I did not want to live there the rest of my life. Without any type of college degree and with limited work experience, my job opportunities were minimal.

My mother administered the Armed Services Vocational Aptitude Battery (ASVAB) tests to high school students. New military recruits take the ASVAB test to determine whether they're qualified to enlist in the United States Armed Forces. Through her work, my mother knew several local recruiters from the various military branches.

The Air Force recruiter in my town happened to be my neighbor, and I visited with him about his experience in the Air Force. Also, my best friend was a couple years older than me, and he was already an active-duty airman at the time. I talked with him about what he liked about serving, the challenges he had faced, and any other advice he was willing to share with me. Based on my discussions with my best friend and the recruiter, I decided to commit to four years in the United States Air Force (USAF). I was excited about my decision and also anxious about what I was getting myself into.

Less than 1 percent of US citizens currently serve in the military. Looking at the veteran population, only about 6 percent of US citizens have ever served. Given the small percentage of US citizens with military experience, it can sometimes be difficult for young adults to talk to people who are currently serving or who have served.

Back in the 1950s, '60s, and '70s, there were many more active-duty military personnel, so there was a much greater chance that a young person would have a family member, neighbor, or acquaintance to talk to about their experiences. Since the number of active-duty personnel is much lower today, I hope that this book can take the place of such chats.

I served for four years, and my experience is naturally going to be different from that of others. I had friends who ended up making the military their career and retiring from it after decades of experience. However, the purpose of this book is to present a post-high school option other than attending college right away or going to work in your hometown. Those are both great options, but the military was the right choice for me—and it may be for you.

"It takes courage to grow and become who you really are." - E.E. Cummings

Chapter 2. The Branches

The US military has six branches of service: the Army, Navy, Air Force, Coast Guard, Marine Corps, and Space Force. The Army National Guard and the Air National Guard are reserve components of their respective branches and operate in part under state authority. For this book, I will focus on the six active-duty branches.

While the requirements to join are similar in each, they differ slightly in results from the Armed Services Vocational Aptitude Battery (ASVAB) test, fitness levels, and age limits. You must be at least eighteen years of age (or seventeen with parental consent) to enlist in any branch of the military. You must also be a US citizen or have a permanent resident card; live in the United States; and speak, write, and read English fluently. You must have a high school diploma to enlist, though in certain situations, a GED is accepted. There are some disqualifying factors, such as criminal history, age, physical requirements, drug abuse, or certain medical conditions. All the service branches have their own websites, which specify their requirements. You could also reach out to a military recruiter if you have a unique situation and are concerned it could disqualify you.

Below is a brief description of the six active-duty branches of the military so you can better understand when each branch was established, what their mission is, and the size of each organization.

The United States Army was founded in 1775 as part of the Department of Defense. As of 2022, it had 463,083 active-duty members. According to the US Army's website, their main purpose is "to deploy, fight and win our nations' wars by providing ready, prompt and sustained land dominance by Army forces across the full spectrum of conflict as part of the joint force."

The United States Marines were founded in 1798 as part of the Department of Defense and had 180,958 active-duty members in 2022. According to their website, the US Marine Corps' mission is "In essence our nation is that purpose. In our world, in ourselves, and in our way, there are conflicts, challenges, and obstacles that must be fought confidently and defeated convincingly for our nation to prevail. These looming battles come in many forms and occur on many fronts, but each comes down to a critical choice: to demand victory or accept defeat. To pull together or fall apart. To give in or cave in. It is a decision each marine conveys to our nation with each battle won."

The United States Navy was founded in 1775 and is also part of the Department of Defense. In 2022, it had 349,593 active-duty members. The Navy's mission statement is: "The United States is a maritime nation, and the U.S. Navy protects America at sea. Alongside our allies and partners, we defend freedom, preserve economic prosperity, and keep the seas open and free. Our nation is engaged in long-term competition. To defend American interests around the globe, the U.S. Navy must remain prepared to execute our timeless role, as directed by Congress and the President."

The United States Air Force was founded in 1947 and is part of the Department of Defense. It had 328,820 active-duty members in 2022. According to their website, United States Air Force's mission is "To fly, fight and win- airpower anytime, anywhere. Whether full time, part time, in or out of uniform, everyone who serves plays a critical role in helping us achieve mission success."

The United States Coast Guard was founded in 1775, is part of the Department of Homeland Security, and had 40,558 active-duty members as of 2022. According to their website, the United States Coast Guard provides national security and search and rescue for America's waterways, seas, and coastlines. The US Coast Guard manages six major operational mission programs: Maritime Law Enforcement,

Maritime Response, Maritime Prevention, Maritime Transportation Systems Management, Maritime Security Operations, and Defense Operations.

The United States Space Force was founded in 2019. It is part of the Department of the Air Force and in 2022 had 8,600 active-duty members. It is the smallest branch of the military. According to its website, the Space Force is "responsible for organizing, training, and equipping Guardians to conduct global space operations that enhance the way our joint and coalition forces fight, while also offering decision makers military options to achieve national objectives."

I recommend you do additional research on your own, learning more about each branch as well as different career paths that each might offer. This can be accomplished through online searches, visiting your local library, or talking to active military personnel or veterans that you know. After you have completed your own research, the next step would be to contact a local recruiter.

"There are far better things ahead than we ever leave behind." – C.S. Lewis

Chapter 3. The Process

If you aren't sure where your nearest recruiter is located, you can look online.

When talking to a recruiter, remember that one of their main responsibilities is to convince qualified candidates to join their branch of service. Recruiters have quotas to meet. They are expected to get a certain number of prospects to enlist in their branch. So, be prepared for a recruiter to put some pressure on you to sign up. Be confident when you go into a meeting with a recruiter and have the mindset that you are interviewing them just as much as they are interviewing you. Remember: you do not have to do anything in your first few meetings, even though you may feel some pressure. Your goal for your initial meetings should be to get all your questions answered and learn more about that branch of service. I recommend bringing a notepad with all the questions you have thought of since starting this journey. The recruiter will share all the positives they have experienced in the military. Be sure to ask them about any negatives or cons there may be to joining the military. Any job, whether military or civilian, has pros and cons associated with them. If the recruiter says there are no cons to joining, that is a red flag.

All the branches have similar positions like cooks, administration, police officers, information technology, intelligence analysts, medical professionals, construction workers, mechanics, and recruiters, just to name a few. However, some branches have more specific jobs, like infantry soldiers, fire control officers, and divers. All the branches have their own special force units.

All branches have extensive websites where you can find some military occupational specialties (MOS) that might interest you. Your recruiter will also know about opportunities that may suit you.

The more information you can share with your recruiter during your meeting, the easier it will be to narrow down opportunities you qualify for.

Dress appropriately for your meeting with your recruiter. You do not need to wear a suit, but I would not recommend wearing shorts and a T-shirt, either. You should wear what you would for a job interview and make sure you are on time for your meeting. Being on time is a must in the military, as you will learn in basic training. Make sure your phone is on silent mode or leave it in your car. Remember, you would not answer a call during a job interview.

When the recruiter asks questions about your past, including your medical history or any past involvement with law enforcement, always be honest. If you enlist, you will have to undergo a physical and your medical history will be reviewed, so lying at this stage will not help. Also, when they conduct a background check, any past interactions with law enforcement (if you have any) will be discovered.

The military has a zero-tolerance policy for illegal drugs or abusing prescription drugs. If you have used illegal drugs in the past, again, be honest. Some branches will grant waivers on prior drug use. However, there are several factors they take into consideration before granting such a waiver, including the type of drug used, age at the time of use, and any related law violations.

Even if your meeting with the recruiter goes well, I recommend not committing to anything that day. There are a few reasons for this. You may want to visit a recruiter from another branch to see what options they can offer you. Even if you're set on this particular branch, take sufficient time to go over the recruiter's answers. Spend a week or two evaluating pros, cons, and your options. I also recommend that you tell the recruiter that you'll need time to consider your decision; that way, they won't call you in the next day or two. Also, ask the recruiter for the phone numbers of two or three former recruits that they worked with. Those recruits who are now active-duty military could answer any questions you have about the enlistment process or the military itself.

Some recruiters will speak highly of their branch and negatively about other branches. They may also tell you that their branch does not have the occupation you are looking to get into. Make sure you reach out to recruiters for other branches and confirm that any information you receive is accurate.

An important question to ask each recruiter is what their branch's minimum service obligation is. Typically, each branch will require a minimum of a six-year commitment. The first four years will be on active duty, with the remaining years in the inactive ready reserves. In the reserves, you return to living in the civilian world, but you can be called back up to active duty at any time. This typically happens when a large conflict breaks out. For example, a year after I left the military, my father received a call from my former squadron commander, asking him to let me know that there was a possibility I could be called back up to active duty due to a conflict that was escalating at the time. After that initial call, he did not call back, so I did not have to report for duty.

After you finish your research and feel ready to make the commitment to join the armed forces, you should set up another meeting with your recruiter. The main purpose of this meeting is to ask any lingering questions you may have and let them know that you are ready to start the process of joining the military.

Your recruiter will coordinate with a military entrance processing station (MEPS) to set up an appointment for you to take the Armed Services Vocational Aptitude Battery (ASVAB) test. The ASVAB is a multiple-choice test that helps determine the careers for which you are best suited. You may have already taken this test in high school. If this is the case, let your recruiter know, and they can see if your results are still valid. If you do need to take the ASVAB test, I recommend buying a study guide either from a bookstore or online to help you study for it. There are several options to choose from.

The ASVAB consists of different subject-matter areas such as general science, arithmetic reasoning, word knowledge, paragraph comprehension, math knowledge, electronics information, mechanical comprehension, and shop information and assembling objects. It typically takes about three hours to complete. Make sure you get enough sleep the night before the exam and arrive at the testing site early so you are not rushed.

The next step would be to go through a physical, which typically consists of taking your height and weight; examining your hearing and visual abilities; testing for drug and alcohol use; collecting urine and blood samples for analysis; and reviewing your medical history with a physician. Your recruiter would likely have already asked you to fill out DD Form 2807-2, which includes questions about your current medical status and past medical history.

If you successfully pass the ASVAB test and your physical, the next step would typically be to meet with a MEPS career counselor. This counselor will review your ASVAB test results and share career options that might be a good fit for you as well as for the military branch you selected.

One of the MEPS career counselor's objectives is filling open positions with qualified applicants. So, they may try to persuade you to go into a specific field. You do not have to accept a career you are not comfortable with, as this would not be good for you or for the military branch you selected.

Ultimately, your score on the ASVAB test will determine if you qualify for the military occupational specialty you are interested in. Do not be disappointed if you do not score well in a certain section, which disqualifies you for that position. There is likely another occupation you would be a good candidate for.

Originally, I thought I was going to be a police officer in the United States Air Force. However, when I met with my career counselor, he said my test scores were quite high in certain areas and encouraged me to explore some other Air Force Specialty Codes (AFSC). He said that being a military police officer is an honorable position, but there were some other AFSCs that I qualified for as well. The one that really intrigued me was the intelligence field. As we discussed my options, I decided to become an intelligence operations specialist.

Once you decide on your future career path, you're ready to take the oath of enlistment. The oath of enlistment is conducted by a military officer. The officer will stand in front of you, with the US flag in the background, and ask you to raise your right hand and repeat: "I, [state your name], do solemnly swear (or affirm) that I will support and defend the Constitution of the United States against all enemies, foreign and domestic; that I will bear true faith and allegiance to the same; and that I will obey the orders of the President of the United States and the orders of the officers appointed over me, according to regulations and the Uniform Code of Military Justice. So help me God."

Next, you will set a date for when you will report to basic training.

In my case, a month after I took the oath of enlistment, my parents drove me to the nearest MEPS, and I spent the night with another recruit. I was so nervous that night that I barely slept. The next morning, I was on a plane to basic training in San Antonio, Texas.

I was what is called a "direct ship." This means that once I went through the process at MEPS, I knew I would be going to basic training in a short time frame. The other option most branches of service offer is called the delayed entry program (DEP). The DEP allows recruits to report to basic training at a future date, typically within one year of taking the oath of enlistment. Some common reasons a recruit may choose the DEP option are not meeting weight or fitness standards, prior commitments like college classes or a wedding, or the job they want is not yet available.

"Courage is the most important of all the virtues because without courage, you can't practice any other virtue consistently." - *Maya Angelou*

Chapter 4. Basic Training

Once you commit to joining the military, I recommend that you begin physically and mentally preparing.

Start setting your alarm and getting up at five A.M. This will help you adjust to basic training, where you will typically be in formation by five or five-thirty A.M. and have activities until you are in bed with the lights out at nine P.M.

If you do not currently run or jog regularly, I would encourage you to start walking every day. Build up to at least two or three miles a day. Eventually, you should be able to jog that distance before you leave for basic training. When I was in basic training, a large part of my day was spent marching and doing drills where we were running and moving constantly.

You will also do a lot of push-ups and sit-ups in basic training, so the more you can practice both ahead of time, the more prepared you will be. You will likely be required to do more push-ups and sit-ups than pull-ups, but I would still recommend that you have at least practiced doing pull-ups, as you will be asked to do some throughout basic training.

In my experience, the recruits that struggled the most in basic training were the ones who did not physically prepare beforehand.

Also, get in the habit of drinking a lot of water and eating healthy foods, as this will fuel your workouts and improve your overall health.

Before you leave for basic training, you should pack a small "carry-on" suitcase. This should include personal items like underwear, athletic socks, running shoes, bras (for women), a few changes of civilian clothes, and a padlock for your locker. You will mostly be wearing fatigues and workout clothes the military provides, so you do not need to pack a bunch of clothes. Make sure to pack toiletries like a toothbrush, toothpaste, deodorant, bodywash, shampoo, hand soap, razors, shaving cream, and, for women, feminine hygiene items and hair ties that match your hair color. I highly recommend that you do not bring any tobacco products, alcohol, nonprescription drugs, weapons, obscene materials, or expensive items like a laptop, camera, or jewelry. Also, pack your current driver's license, social security card, immunization card, high school transcript, prescription drug information, and bank account information for your direct-depot form.

My recruiter shared a list of what *not* to bring to basic training with me, but several of my peers did not receive this information. When we arrived, we were instructed to empty our bags on our beds, and the drill instructors publicly berated the individuals who brought inappropriate items. One of the recruits in my group brought several provocative pictures of his girlfriend. A drill instructor passed the pictures around, which embarrassed the recruit, before confiscating them. Another recruit brought a carton of cigarettes. The drill instructor grabbed them and demanded, "What made you think you would be able to smoke these?" They were also confiscated. In general, keep any personal items you bring to basic training to a minimum.

Before you leave for basic training, you should decide which family member or friend you want to pay any bills you have during this period and deal with any other obligations you will not be able to handle when you are gone.

All your activities will be scheduled in military time. There is no A.M. or P.M. in military time, as numbers are not reused; instead, each hour has its own number. Any given time of day is expressed in four digits. The day in military time begins at midnight, which is 0000, pronounced "zero hundred hours." You add one hundred for each hour, so one A.M. is 0100, two A.M. is 0200 hours, and so forth. Noon in military time is 1200, and one P.M. is 1300. The day ends at 11:59 civilian time, which is 2359 military time.

Basic training differs between the different branches. Some of the activities that are consistent across branches include turning in enlistment paperwork and receiving medical and dental exams. You will get any immunizations you need as well as your uniforms and training gear. If you are a male, you will receive a short, regulation haircut. Women can keep their hair long, provided it can be worn within regulation requirements.

I will not get into the specific training you will go through, as each branch is different. Your recruiter will be able to give you more specifics. All branches will have physical training, field exercises, and classroom time.

Basic training is designed to push recruits to their mental and physical limits as well as instill discipline. You will learn about the different military ranks and how to properly salute superior officers. You will complete intense physical activities like running and obstacle courses, and you will likely learn how to properly use military weapons. You will also spend a lot of time in the classroom, learning about the military in general as well as your specific branch of service.

One of my most vivid memories of basic training is our drill instructors circling around us while we ate in the chow hall, telling us to hurry up and clean our plates. Mealtimes are not for socializing; they are a time to refuel your body to prepare for the next activity of the day.

In many ways, basic training is a very psychological mind game. My best advice in dealing with this is to keep a good mindset about the whole experience. Everyone will get yelled at during basic training, even when you do something right. If you are in line for a drill, watch your classmates as they perform a certain drill or exercise and learn from their example if they do something right or get yelled at. Then, when it is your turn, you have a better idea of the expectation.

Never talk back to a drill instructor or disagree with them, as you will likely be disciplined. Always address your drill instructor as "sir" or "ma'am." Remember that one of a drill instructor's main responsibilities is to mentally and physically prepare recruits to serve their country.

Be prepared to be homesick, as that is a common feeling. Keep in mind that this is a very short period of your life. When I was in basic training, the trainee who slept in the bunk right next to me cried every night. After a couple nights of this, I talked to him and learned that he missed his wife, whom he had just married a few weeks before he shipped off to basic training. I would not recommend getting married right before you go to basic training, as your contact with the civilian world is limited during this time. The drill instructors will keep your cell phones locked up during the week, and you will occasionally be allowed to call home for a short period of time, usually on the weekends. You will not have access to computers, the internet, or social media during basic training, but you will be allowed to send and receive letters through the mail.

The very small number of trainees who are not following instructions, having difficulties in the classroom, or struggling with the physical aspect of training may be "phased back." Being phased back means that they will be placed with another group of trainees who are just beginning the training process, which will extend their time in basic training.

A few recruits in my class were phased back due to not being physically or mentally prepared. However, this was a very small percentage of our group.

Even though basic training will likely be the most physically and mentally difficult event in a young recruit's life, only roughly 15 percent fail basic training, with each service having a slightly different range. When you get anxious, frustrated, or sad, remember that this is only about eight-to-ten weeks of your life. After I finished basic training, I was in the best physical condition of my life and was mentally stronger.

At some point during basic training, you will fill out your "dream sheet," which is where you list your top choices for the location of your first duty assignment. The likelihood of getting your first preference is slim, but the military will look at your occupation, see what base(s) have a need for your position, and at least take your "dream sheet" into consideration. In my case, I put down several cities near beaches. I ended up at Offutt Air Force Base in Nebraska, which was the closest military base to where I grew up. Needless to say, it did not have a beach.

Once you successfully complete basic training, you will attend graduation. I was so excited to have gotten through this difficult process and that my parents were able to fly down to San Antonio, Texas, to attend the ceremony. As part of the graduation ceremony, we had a graduation parade, where we marched as a squadron in our dress blues.

After the graduation ceremony, I was able to spend about six hours with my parents before I had to report back to base. They told me that they were incredibly proud of me. I felt like I had a purpose in life again.

The next day, I was on a bus heading to San Angelo, Texas, to complete the next phase of my military commitment, which was technical school.

"Be brave. Take risks. Nothing can substitute experience." - Paulo Coelho

Chapter 5. Technical School

Completing basic training is a great accomplishment. Next, you will attend tech school, where you will learn the skills you need to execute your job. Tech schools can take as little as six weeks to as much as over one year to complete, depending on the specialty. As an intelligence analyst in the US Air Force, my tech school was a twelve-week program.

Tech schools consist of phases. In basic training, you cannot leave the base until you graduate, and then, you are only allowed off the base for a few hours. The military wants to slowly phase new soldiers back into the civilian world. In my case, our class at tech school was not allowed off base for the first two weeks, and during that time, our regimen was much like the end of basic training. One difference was that the classroom instruction in technical school was focused on our specialty. In basic training, we instead learned more general topics, like the history of the military, leadership principles, and teamwork.

Another difference is that in technical school, you will be able to watch TV, make phone calls more frequently, have access to the internet, and play basketball or other sports with your classmates. You will likely live in a dorm setting, rather than barracks. Beginning in week three, we could go off base for a limited time, but we were still required to wear our military uniforms. Then, in week four, we could leave the base without wearing our uniforms.

Technical school is a very serious period in the military's eyes because it is where they train you to become well-versed in your career so you can succeed in the future and be an important member of the greatest military force in the world. With that in mind, I recommend that when you are given the privilege to leave base, stay focused on the reason you are there. A few members of my class got in trouble for things they did off base, like underage drinking, drinking too much for those of legal age, and getting into fights. This sort of behavior can result in severe discipline up to a dishonorable discharge. You do not want to erase everything you have accomplished up to this point. Plus, if you get written up for something you did at tech school, those records will follow you to your next assignment.

Members of the military are subject to many rules, regulations, and laws. In addition to having to obey the laws of the United States, military personnel are also subject to a special set of laws called the Uniform Code of Military Justice (UCMJ). The UCMJ was enacted by Congress and applies to all active-duty personnel. If a service member commits an offense that involves the civilian or international community, the military may choose to let civilian authorities handle the case. However, a member of the military may be tried for the same crime in both civilian and military courts under separate charges.

While in tech school, make sure to keep your room clean and take your trash out daily, as you will have room inspections.

One significant benefit of technical school in the military versus technical school or college in the civilian world is that there is no cost to you. You receive your education for free, and you will be paid military wages while in school.

My specialty required a great deal of time in the classroom. Depending on your specialty, you might receive college credits from your tech school. As I mentioned in a prior chapter, I joined the military because I was not prepared for college as an eighteen-year-old and was more focused on other things. However, after successfully completing basic training and with the support of my instructors, I regained the confidence and discipline I needed to successfully pass tech school.

You will become close to your tech school classmates because you will be with them at all times, just like in basic training.

However, in tech school, your classmates are training in the same field as you, and there is a good chance you will join a few or many of them at your first duty assignment or at future duty assignments.

When I completed tech school in 1990, the Persian Gulf War was just beginning. Many members of my class assumed we would be deployed to the Middle East to support the war through our specialty. However, ten members of our class ended up being sent to Offutt Air Force Base in Omaha, Nebraska, for our first duty assignment. At the time, Offutt Air Force Base was the home of Strategic Air Command and had eight thousand active-duty members and civilian support staff on base. It was one of the largest Air Force bases in the world. Some of my other classmates were deployed to much smaller bases throughout the country.

Upon completion of your technical school, there will be a graduation. Not all technical schools allow family members to attend tech school graduation. Once you graduate from technical school, you will typically be given around ten days of leave. This is a good time to go home and visit friends and family who will be excited to see you and hear about your recent accomplishments.

The next step in your journey is to report to your first duty assignment. This is an exciting time in your life. You have successfully completed basic training as well as your technical school, and you are now ready to continue learning and applying your skills in the military.

"Education is the one thing no one can take away from you." – B.B. King

Chapter 6. First Duty Assignment

Now that you have completed both basic training and your technical school, you're ready to get settled in your new home for the next few years.

Typically, when you arrive at your first duty station, the first place you will go is the reception or administrative office to give them a copy of your orders. The staff will let you know where you will be residing on base. They will also give you a map of the base and go over the location of some of the main buildings, like the chow hall and where your unit is located.

You will generally meet your new coworkers and start learning about your duties the following day. Many of your coworkers at your first duty station will become lifelong friends, as you will work, eat and live with them. You will also have more freedom now, much like before you went to basic training and tech school. However, when you are in the military, you are held to a higher standard in your personal life than civilians. For example, you must keep your hair trimmed to a certain length, you may have more random drug tests than a civilian would for their job, your clothes must be ironed a certain way, and depending on your job, you may have to maintain certain physical fitness requirements.

Typically, you are required to live on base for the first couple years of your military career in a barrack or dorm. Many bases also have married housing units if you are married. After three or four years and depending on your rank and branch, you may have the opportunity to live off base. If this is the case, the military will provide you with a housing allowance to help subsidize your off-base living costs. You will be able to have your own car on base and drive it off base, unlike when you were in basic training and possibly also in technical school.

As I mentioned earlier, my first duty assignment was Offutt Air Force Base. Even though I grew up in a town of thirty thousand people, being assigned to a base with over eight thousand people was a bit overwhelming at first. That is a lot of service members in a fairly small physical area!

I quickly learned that even when I was outside my work environment or dorm room, I needed to be ready to salute a commissioned or warrant officer. Since Offutt Air Force base was the headquarters of Strategic Air Command at the time, there were thousands of officers from all branches working at or visiting the base. On one occasion in my first week, I did not salute an officer; this was unintentional, and I didn't realize he was an officer until I had passed him. He stopped me and yelled at me, and I made sure that did not happen again.

Once I had been on base for a few weeks and had gotten my bearings, I really enjoyed being there. I rarely left the base in the first month or so because the chow halls were so nice and my dorm was newer. Also, they had several barbershops, a grocery store, a gas station, a hospital, gyms, dry cleaners, and other essential facilities on base.

Offutt Air Force Base had a strip of historic houses, known as "General's Row," which housed generals who worked on the base. Back in the 1990s, there were fifteen or so houses on "General's Row." Some military bases have a colonel as their base commander, so having so many generals at one location was unique.

I was an intelligence operations team specialist, and I worked in the 24/7-watch command center. One of my position's main responsibilities was to receive real-time intelligence information from the Defense Intelligence Agency as well as the Central Intelligence Agency and distribute sensitive information to other military personnel with the proper clearances to assist them in their duties. To do this, I needed the highest security clearance, which is Top Secret/SCI (sensitive compartmented information) Clearance. Data that has a Top Secret/SCI clearance typically involves national security.

The background check for this type of clearance can take anywhere from three months up to a year to complete and is very thorough. Typically, the Department of Defense will go back at least ten years in your life history and conduct interviews with schoolteachers, friends, neighbors, prior employers, coaches, and any other person you had regular contact with. They want to make sure you are trustworthy, reliable, honest, and mentally competent. Also, they want to make sure you are not involved with any illegal drug use, are not a dual citizen, have not been convicted of a felony in the past ten years, do not have financial problems, and do not have ties to any foreign country. Background checks for security clearances can range from a few hundred dollars up to a few thousand dollars. A background check for a Top-Secret clearance can be five thousand dollars or more. Fortunately, the military pays for these.

In my case, a few friends, a former teacher, and a neighbor all informed me that they had been contacted by the relevant agency conducting my background check and asked many questions regarding my character, honesty, and integrity as an individual.

If your job requires a security clearance and you successfully pass the background check, this designation is very favorably viewed by the civilian community when you eventually leave the military and apply for a civilian job. I am currently a president/CEO for a community bank in Iowa, and my military experience and security clearance were the most significant factors in obtaining my first banking job as a commercial lender twenty-five years ago. You do not need a security clearance to become a banker, but my hiring manager said that those qualifications set me apart from the other candidates. At the time, I was competing against recent college graduates with business degrees or some banking experience as a teller or internship. I have a BA degree from the University of

Iowa in sociology and did not have banking experience.

On-the-job training at your first duty station will be invaluable to you as you progress in your military career as well as in the civilian world. I was fortunate to have some very knowledgeable supervisors who taught me leadership skills, public speaking skills, and ways to work more efficiently. My supervisors were often busy with their own tasks, so I appreciated that they took the time to train me, get me involved, and help me grow and become a valuable member of the team.

There will be times at your first duty station where you might second-guess yourself, since you will be one of the new trainees. Remember that all your superiors were in your shoes at one time. Also, keep in mind that teamwork is important in any job in all branches of the military. No one person can accomplish missions by themselves. Therefore, your supervisors and peers will be there to assist in your learning process. Depending on the size of your unit, you will eventually be mentoring the new trainees who come in.

Depending on where you are first stationed, once you are familiar with your base, I recommend visiting with your peers and asking about local places they have visited and maybe clubs or activities they are involved with in the civilian community. Several of my peers and I visited different clubs and gyms around Omaha and met many civilians who became our friends.

You will also eventually receive furlough, which is like vacation time, which you can use to take a trip somewhere or go see family.

Typically, a member of the military will spend two-to-four years at their first duty station. That is a relatively brief period of one's life, so take advantage of the opportunity to explore your new community. There are obviously better locations to be stationed than others. Try to make the best of your situation, whatever it is, and remember that the longer you stay in the military, the more opportunities you will have to see the world. If you decide to make the military a career, there is a good chance that you will have the opportunity to be stationed overseas at some point or take part in a deployment.

If you decide to only serve out your initial service commitment, you may well stay at your initial duty station for the duration. However, if you chose to stay in the military for longer than that, you will likely receive orders to report to a new duty station at some point. The good news is that once you move to your second duty station, you will have more knowledge and experience. You will no longer be the trainee and will likely be starting to train or manage others.

"To be successful one must be willing to learn and apply new concepts and not be afraid of change." - Craig R. Barrett

Chapter 7. Your Second Duty Station

If you decide to serve your country for only your initial commitment, there is a good chance that you will serve out your term at one location. However, if your branch needs your specialty at another base, you could be transferred before your commitment is completed.

In my case, I had been at Offutt Air Force Base for two years when my commanding officer informed me that I was being transferred to Hurlburt Airfield, located in Florida. Unlike when you are offered a job in the civilian world, where you have a choice to accept the position or not, in the military, you do not have a choice.

After this meeting, I had a lot of questions and thoughts about what this meant. I had established a network of friends, was succeeding in my job, and was comfortable with living near Omaha. I was close enough to home to regularly visit family and friends in my hometown. On the flip side, I had wanted to be stationed near a beach from the start of my military career, and this transfer would give me this chance, as Hurlburt Field is right by a beach.

Hurlburt Airfield houses the Air Force Special Operations Command, and once I did some research on Hurlburt Airfield and their mission, I became more excited. The base houses the Strategic Special Force units of the United States Air Force, which meant there was a very good chance that I would be deployed to support our country if we engaged in a conflict. After transferring to Hurlburt Field, I did end up deploying to a couple conflicts, which I will discuss more in a later chapter.

Moving can be mentally challenging, especially when you are moving thousands of miles away. The military does a great job of coordinating and paying for your move, which is very helpful. Also, the management team at your new squadron will be in contact with you prior to your move to serve as a resource. Still, I highly recommend that you do as much research on the base you are transferring to as you can.

Back in 1992, when I made this transfer, the internet did not exist, and I did not do enough research beforehand. So, when I arrived, I was a little shocked and lonely at first. I missed my network of friends, and my squadron was much smaller than it was at my prior duty assignment. The number of active-duty members and the physical size of the base were much smaller than Offutt. The dorm I was assigned was very old compared to the new dorms I lived in at Offutt. When I was not working, I explored the nearby towns and spent time relaxing on the beaches. Oskaloosa County, Florida, is very beautiful and has some of the best beaches in the country. After a few months, I became closer to some of the people I worked with, and this assignment ended up being a very beneficial move for me.

When I was stationed at Hurlburt, I was assigned to support the 16th Special Operations Squadron. I worked alongside a few officers to brief the crew of the AC-130 gunship aircraft. The AC-130's purpose was to provide close air support for many of the other branches' special operation units. If the United States was involved in a post-Vietnam War conflict, there is a good chance the AC-130 crews were there.

After I had lived on base for a year, I had the opportunity to move off base. I talked to a friend who also had this opportunity, and we found a duplex to share. We received a basic allowance for housing that supplemented our monthly rent. I enjoyed living off base, as it provided more mental freedom for me.

There are pros and cons to living off base. Some pros are that you can choose your housing, experience more of the local community, have more separation between work and your personal life, and build equity if you purchase a property. On the other hand, some cons are that you may have to supplement the difference between your rent and the basic housing allowance you receive. You also have to go through the base's security gates more frequently, and you may have issues with breaking a lease if you receive orders to deploy to a conflict or another base.

Depending on your military occupational specialty, your role could differ slightly at each base you are stationed at. In my role at my first duty station, I stayed Stateside, and all my professional interactions were with my squadron. At my second duty station, I was able to work with different squadrons as well as different branches and was deployed a couple times.

"Develop a passion for learning. If you do, you will never cease to grow." - Anthony J. D'Angelo

Chapter 8. TDY and Deployment

The biggest difference between military deployments and temporary duty assignments (TDY) is the length of the orders.

TDY is an assignment or travel to another location that typically lasts a couple days up to 180 days. During my four-year enlistment, I only had one TDY, which involved being sent to MacDill Air Force Base in Tampa, Florida, for some training. Depending on your specialty, you may have several TDYs during your time in the military.

There are several benefits that come with TDYs beyond the learning experience, such as per diem pay, which is an allowance to cover your meals, lodging, and incidental expenses, as well as the opportunity to meet other service members on different bases. If you receive TDY orders that exceed thirty days, make sure you coordinate with one of your coworkers or friends to check on your local affairs, such as checking on your apartment if you live off base and picking up your mail.

Deployment is the movement of armed forces outside the continental United States. Deployment is not restricted to combat, as units can be deployed for humanitarian aid, increased security, or to evacuate US citizens from a dangerous region. Typically, deployments last between ninety days and a year and a half. When someone receives deployment orders, it is common to feel many emotions, especially anxiety.

I remember the first time I was told I was being deployed like it was yesterday. I went to a movie with some friends, and when I arrived home at my off-base duplex around ten P.M., there was a message on my answering message; cell phones were not common at the time. The message was from my squadron commander. He instructed me to pack my duffle bags and be at the base by five A.M. the following morning. After hearing that message, I strongly suspected that I was being deployed somewhere.

When I arrived on base early the next morning, we were briefed by our superior officer, who told us that we were being deployed to Somalia, a country in Africa, to support the Battle of Mogadishu. We deployed a few hours after the briefing.

Once we got this news, I felt a little overwhelmed, as I had never traveled outside the United States before, let alone to a hostile area. On the other hand, I was excited, as this was what I had signed up for when I joined the military. I was fortunate to have a few service members who were veterans of prior military engagements outside the United States joining me on this trip. Their knowledge, confidence, and experience were invaluable to me.

It is very important to always have all your affairs in order if you are ever deployed, because depending on your role and where you are deploying, there may be a very short window of time between receiving your orders and shipping out. I was also instructed not to contact family or friends and discuss where I was being deployed. This is a typical practice, as this information could be used by an enemy to jeopardize military members, operations, and strategies.

My squadron was deployed to provide air support, as eighteen US soldiers had been killed during an incident later referred to as "Black Hawk Down." On my flight to Somalia, I was anxious, scared, excited, and curious. This was the first time I would be outside the continental United States as well as the first time representing my country in a conflict.

Once we landed, my squadron, along with squadrons from several other branches of the military, including the US Navy and US Army, met as a group in a large airport hangar, and we were all briefed by a one-star general who oversaw the mission. He told us some of the basics about the region and what the overall mission was from a macro level.

Over the next few weeks, I worked alongside my superior officer, who was a captain. The captain and I met daily with a Central Intelligence Agency officer who worked alongside the Defense Intelligence Agency to provide us with real-time intelligence on the enemy forces led by warlord Mohamed Aided. We then briefed the AC-130 gunship air crews, along with the other units they supported, such as the Navy Seals and Army Rangers, and strategically planned our missions.

I continued to feel many of the emotions I'd experienced on the flight over to Somalia for several weeks. However, I was also focused and engaged on my work. I was assisting with a real-world conflict and felt proud to be part of a team representing the United States. My superior had graduated from the Air Force Academy and already had deployment experience, as he served in the Persian Gulf War. His experience invaluable to me, and I learned a lot from his ability to decipher complex information and communicate the pertinent pieces to the relevant joint forces to carry out their mission.

We ended up being in the theater for several months. To say I, a twenty-one-year-old, was overwhelmed is an understatement.

When you deploy to a conflict, you become close with the troops deployed with you. Whether you are a pilot, mechanic, special force operator, tank operator, or medic, everyone is there to support each other. All roles are critical for the mission's success.

While the daily stress of being in a hostile area cannot be ignored, you do receive several benefits from being deployed. You will receive per diem pay and possibly combat or hazard pay, which can amount to double or more what your regular salary is. The experience itself is also invaluable for your future military career, as you will likely be called upon in future conflicts, and your teammates will rely on your experience. Also, the resulting leadership and teamwork experience are invaluable for your future, whether you stay in the military and make it your career or return to the civilian world. Also, in my case, being deployed was the first time I was able to work with members from all the other branches of the military as well as meet and befriend some soldiers from other countries who were part of our United Nations force.

Depending on your military occupational specialty, you could face challenges such as loneliness, anxiety, or depression. Medical specialists are deployed to every conflict, and you can visit them if any of these emotions escalate. The troops you are deployed with will likely be experiencing these same thoughts, so you will have a good support system. Should these feelings persist when you return to your regular duty station, there are support systems in place to help you.

If you decide to make the military your career, there is a good chance you will deploy to some country, whether for a military conflict or humanitarian effort.

I ended up deploying once more for the Bosnian War, and since I had already deployed previously, I was more prepared for that conflict. The Bosnian War was an international armed conflict that took place in Bosnia and Herzegovina between 1992 and 1995.

I am glad I was able to experience both of these conflicts, as the experience strengthened my confidence and leadership skills and enabled me to gain some long-term friendships.

"You never really know how strong you are until being strong is the only choice you have." - Author Unknown

Chapter 9. Military Benefits

"Basic pay" is the standard term the military uses for the compensation you receive semimonthly for your services to your country. You might sometimes hear that members of the military are not paid well; personally, I consider that a myth. If the basic pay alone is a deterrent to you joining the military, you need to look at the full compensation package you will receive even as a new service member.

Beyond basic pay, the benefits you receive include:

◆Housing or a housing allowance
◆Food
◆Health and dental care
◆Travel
◆Thirty days' paid vacation
◆Advanced training
◆Military exchange stores
◆Access to gyms and sports facilities
◆College tuition benefits
◆Special discounts
◆Home loan benefits

♦Potential enlistment bonus
♦Pension (for career service members)
♦Special pay
♦Patriotism

If you just graduated from high school and have minimal work history, I would encourage you to look at a job opening in your community and compare the pay and benefits they offer to the benefits the military provides. In most situations, you will be further ahead from an overall compensation standpoint by joining the military.

The college tuition benefits alone can be substantial. Of course, at this point, you may not have plans to attend college. I also did not plan to attend college again at the time I enlisted in the military. However, my plans eventually changed, and I am very thankful for the military's financial assistance in accomplishing that goal.

The Post-9/11 GI Bill offers up to forty-eight months of education benefits, including funds for tuition, fees, housing, books, and supplies.

One component of the American dream is being able to purchase a home. One large benefit of being an active-duty member of the military or a veteran is qualifying for a VA loan.

Typically, banks require a 20 percent down payment for first-time home-buyers. If someone does not have that much saved up for a down payment, they would have to pay for private mortgage insurance (PMI). PMI can be expensive, and depending on debt-to-income qualifications, it can sometimes disqualify someone from qualifying for a loan when it is added to their loan payment. VA loans typically require no down payment, offer competitive rates, have limited closing costs, and do not require PMI.

Many decades ago, it was common for companies to provide pensions for long-term employees; today, this practice is less common. However, the military still provides pensions to service members who have served at least twenty years. I have several friends who retired from the military after twenty years, received a nice pension, and were still young enough to work at another job, thus increasing their income.

Another very valuable benefit of serving your country is receiving healthcare benefits for the rest of your life for a minimal cost. Healthcare costs continue to rise, and monthly premiums can be very expensive in the civilian world if your employer does not cover them. Even if you decide to serve just one term, like I did, you will receive free healthcare at VA hospitals.

One priceless benefit is that if or when you enter the civilian job market, you will likely viewed more favorably than a candidate with a similar skill set but without a military background.

When I interviewed for my current position as a bank president, the owner of our bank was familiar with my vast experience in the banking sector but was more interested in talking about my time in the military. I spent four years in the military and almost twenty years in banking, but it was my military experience that sealed my job offer. He valued the discipline and commitment service members demonstrate.

There are also programs, grants, and financial aid for veterans who want to start their own business, whether they are one-term service members or retired after a lengthy career. The Small Business Administration has an Office of Veterans Business Development. Their mission is to maximize the availability, applicability, and usability of all small business programs for veterans, service-disabled veterans, and their dependents.

Many companies provide discounts to active-duty service members and veterans. One example is Lowe's Home Improvement Center. They give active-duty personnel and veterans 10 percent off every purchase.

They also have parking spots reserved for veterans and Purple Heart recipients. I spend a lot of money at Lowe's on landscaping and home improvement items, and these savings really add up over time. Also, many hotel chains and restaurants offer discounts to active-duty members and veterans.

When a veteran dies, they are eligible to receive a military funeral honors ceremony, which includes an honor guard folding and presenting the United States burial flag to the family and playing "Taps." If an active-duty member dies, the family of the deceased receives a significant cash amount called a "death gratuity payment."

These are just a few examples, but as you can see, all these items add up to substantial amounts of money over time. Do not let basic pay alone be a deterrent to joining the military.

"The willingness of American's veterans to sacrifice for our country has earned them our lasting gratitude." - Jeff Miller

Chapter 10. Military Ranks

Each branch of the military has its own ranking system; however, there is some overlap in some branches. The Army, Marine Corps, and Air Force all have their own enlisted military structures. The Navy and Coast Guard mirror each other, and the Space Force mirrors the Air Force.

E-1 is the lowest military rank.

The highest military officer is O-10, which is a five-star general. Only nine generals have ever held that rank. In 1950, General of the Army Omar Bradley was the last general to achieve that rank while still living. General of the Armies George Washington was posthumously recognized with this achievement in 1976.

Enlisted (E) positions in the military require a high school diploma, although with certain exceptions, a GED is acceptable. Officer (O) positions require a four-year degree or equivalent. Enlisted members comprise roughly 80 percent of the United States military, with officers making up the remainder. All positions in the military are essential. The military trains officers to be leaders and managers. They plan the missions, provide orders, and assign tasks. Enlisted members are technical experts in their fields and have the skill sets to complete their tasks.

The military ranking system has been around since the 1700s. The rank system was put in place to make the chain of command clear, with higher-ranking members of the military giving orders to their subordinates. Also, ranking was a way to designate respect, authority, and responsibility.

In the civilian world, if you are given a promotion, you will typically receive a pay raise. Service members also see a pay increase when their rank increases. Your time in service, recommendations from superior officers, and job performance are all factors in how quickly you are promoted up the ranks.

In the Air Force, there is an opportunity called "Below the Zone," which grants top performers an early promotion to E-4. I was fortunate enough to be nominated by my superiors for this achievement. I was excited because not only would I move up in rank sooner than some of my peers, but I would also receive a pay increase. The other branches have similar opportunities for early promotion.

In very rare cases, service members can be reduced in rank due to a failure of performance, committing a crime, bad conduct, or if a service member chooses to switch to another branch of the military.

Enlisted service members who retire at twenty years of active-duty service usually retire at E-7 or E-8 rank, depending on performance and opportunities.

Typically, the military encourages retirement after thirty years of active-duty service. However, if someone has a very senior position, like the Sergeant Major of the Marine Corps, their time in service will likely extend past thirty years.

You will learn the different ranks during basic training. I would encourage you to really understand the different ranks of each branch, because you may end up on a base that houses service members from different branches. My first duty station had members from all branches on base. Understanding the ranking system helped me recognize an individual's rank if I met them outside or passed them in the hallway.

When you start out as an E-1 or E-2, it can be intimidating to see military personnel with several stripes or with different emblems if they are an officer. Just remember that all those people once started out where you are now.

Below, I have included the 2023 pay table for enlisted personnel as well as for officers. This pay table shows basic pay only and does not include the other provided amenities you would be responsible for in the civilian world like housing, food, and health insurance.

Each year, active-duty personnel receive a pay increase at the beginning of the year through the Defense Authorization Act; in 2023, this increase was 4.6 percent. As mentioned before, you may also receive additional income like combat pay, a cost-of-living allowance in high-cost areas, flight pay, sea pay, or temporary duty pay. When I deployed to two conflicts overseas, the additional hazardous duty pay and per diem I received exceeded my basic pay.

Pay Grade	2 or Less	Over 2	Over 3	Over 4	Over 6	Over 8	Over 10	Over 12	Over 14	Over 16	Over 18
2023 Basic Monthly Pay Tables by Grade For Armed Service Members With LESS THAN 20 Yrs of Service											
Officer											
O-8	$ 12,171	$ 12,570	$ 12,834	$ 12,908	$ 13,239	$ 13,790	$ 13,918	$ 14,442	$ 14,592	$ 15,043	$ 15,696
O-7	$ 10,113	$ 10,583	$ 10,800	$ 10,973	$ 11,286	$ 11,595	$ 11,953	$ 12,309	$ 12,667	$ 13,790	$ 14,738
O-6	$ 7,669	$ 8,425	$ 8,978	$ 8,978	$ 9,013	$ 9,399	$ 9,450	$ 9,450	$ 9,987	$ 10,936	$ 11,493
O-5	$ 6,393	$ 7,202	$ 7,700	$ 7,794	$ 8,106	$ 8,292	$ 8,701	$ 9,002	$ 9,389	$ 9,983	$ 10,265
O-4	$ 5,516	$ 6,385	$ 6,812	$ 6,906	$ 7,302	$ 7,726	$ 8,255	$ 8,666	$ 8,951	$ 9,115	$ 9,210
O-3	$ 4,850	$ 5,498	$ 5,934	$ 6,470	$ 6,780	$ 7,120	$ 7,340	$ 7,702	$ 7,890	$ 7,890	$ 7,890
O-2	$ 4,191	$ 4,773	$ 5,497	$ 5,682	$ 5,799	$ 5,799	$ 5,799	$ 5,799	$ 5,799	$ 5,799	$ 5,799
O-1	$ 3,637	$ 3,786	$ 4,577	$ 4,577	$ 4,577	$ 4,577	$ 4,577	$ 4,577	$ 4,577	$ 4,577	$ 4,577
O-3E*				$ 6,470	$ 6,780	$ 7,120	$ 7,340	$ 7,702	$ 8,007	$ 8,182	$ 8,421
O-2E*				$ 5,682	$ 5,799	$ 5,984	$ 6,296	$ 6,537	$ 6,716	$ 6,716	$ 6,716
O-1E*				$ 4,576	$ 4,887	$ 5,068	$ 5,253	$ 5,434	$ 5,682	$ 5,682	$ 5,682
Warrant Officer									© www.savingtoinvest.com		
W-4	$ 5,012	$ 5,392	$ 5,546	$ 5,699	$ 5,961	$ 6,220	$ 6,482	$ 6,878	$ 7,225	$ 7,555	$ 7,824
W-3	$ 4,577	$ 4,768	$ 4,963	$ 5,027	$ 5,232	$ 5,636	$ 6,056	$ 6,254	$ 6,482	$ 6,718	$ 7,142
W-2	$ 4,050	$ 4,433	$ 4,551	$ 4,632	$ 4,895	$ 5,303	$ 5,505	$ 5,705	$ 5,948	$ 6,138	$ 6,311
W-1	$ 3,555	$ 3,937	$ 4,040	$ 4,258	$ 4,516	$ 4,894	$ 5,071	$ 5,318	$ 5,562	$ 5,753	$ 5,929
Enlisted											
E-9	$ -	$ -	$ -	$ -	$ -	$ -	$ 6,056	$ 6,193	$ 6,386	$ 6,569	$ 6,774
E-8	$ -	$ -	$ -	$ -	$ -	$ 4,957	$ 5,176	$ 5,312	$ 5,475	$ 5,651	$ 5,969
E-7	$ 3,446	$ 3,761	$ 3,905	$ 4,096	$ 4,245	$ 4,501	$ 4,645	$ 4,901	$ 5,113	$ 5,258	$ 5,413
E-6	$ 2,981	$ 3,280	$ 3,424	$ 3,565	$ 3,712	$ 4,042	$ 4,171	$ 4,420	$ 4,496	$ 4,552	$ 4,617
E-5	$ 2,731	$ 2,914	$ 3,055	$ 3,199	$ 3,424	$ 3,659	$ 3,851	$ 3,875	$ 3,875	$ 3,875	$ 3,875
E-4	$ 2,504	$ 2,632	$ 2,774	$ 2,915	$ 3,039	$ 3,039	$ 3,039	$ 3,039	$ 3,039	$ 3,039	$ 3,039
E-3	$ 2,260	$ 2,402	$ 2,548	$ 2,548	$ 2,548	$ 2,548	$ 2,548	$ 2,548	$ 2,548	$ 2,548	$ 2,548
E-2	$ 2,149	$ 2,149	$ 2,149	$ 2,149	$ 2,149	$ 2,149	$ 2,149	$ 2,149	$ 2,149	$ 2,149	$ 2,149
E-1**	$ 1,918	$ 1,918	$ 1,918	$ 1,918	$ 1,918	$ 1,918	$ 1,918	$ 1,918	$ 1,918	$ 1,918	$ 1,918

*Special basic pay rate. Applicable to O-1 to O-3 with at least 4 yrs & 1 day of active duty or more than 1460 points as a warrant and/or enl. Member; ** Applies to personnel who have served 4 months or more on active duty.

The rank insignia for each branch for both officers and enlisted personnel is below:

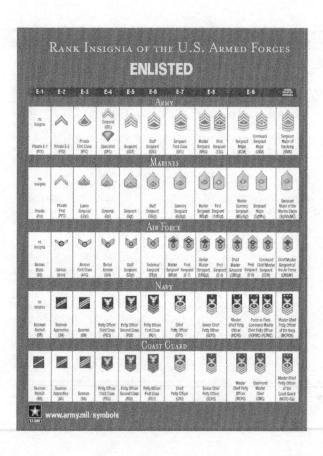

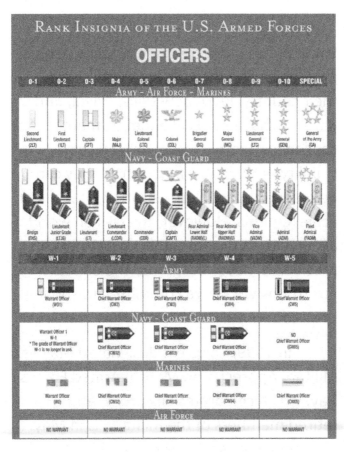

"Success is no accident. It is hard work, perseverance, learning, studying, sacrifice and most of all, love of what you are doing or learning to do." – Pele

Chapter 11. Military Recognition

Some of the more common reasons people give for joining the military are to serve their country, learn new skills, travel, find purpose, have medical benefits, meet challenges, learn a trade, or have job stability. Very few, if any, join so they can be recognized with appreciation, medals, or achievements. However, the civilian world, along with Congress and former American presidents, have recognized the efforts of our troops who have committed to serving their country.

In 1999, Congress designated May as Military Appreciation Month. Armed Forces Day, which celebrates all current and retired members of the military, is in May. Memorial Day is also held in May and honors those who lost their lives defending our country. Veterans Day is always celebrated on November 11 and honors all veterans of the uniformed services who served or are still serving during times of peace as well as war. There are a few other military-related holidays, but these are the more recognized ones.

At many sporting events, active-duty military personnel and veterans are recognized. Also, you are likely to have seen active or past service members marching or on a float in many parades you have attended.

A few years ago, when my son was in high school, the two of us flew to Washington D.C. One of the most incredible experiences we had there was visiting Arlington National Cemetery. Arlington was established during the American Civil War. Over 400,000 people are buried there, most of them being service members who died while on active duty, retired members of the armed forces, and certain military family members. After taking the tour and walking around this sacred place, we sat down on a bench and talked about the history we'd learned and how wonderful it is that this place exists for the service members who made the ultimate sacrifice for their country. More than three million people visit Arlington each year.

Another recognition military members can receive is a military ribbon or medal. Military medals can recognize bravery, heroism, or meritorious service. They can be awarded during peacetime or during war and for recognition of one's successful efforts to continuing to make the United States military the world's premier military.

When I reported for my first day of duty at Offutt, most of the people I passed in the hallways had several more stripes than I did and a lot more ribbons. If you've ever seen a movie with military personnel or seen a senior soldier or officer interviewed on TV, you likely remember all the ribbons and stripes on their uniform. I, in contrast, had one stripe and two ribbons. In basic training, I learned about the ranking system as well as the different ribbons and medals service members can achieve and the significance of each; therefore, I was a little bit in awe.

I was fortunate enough to deploy to a few conflicts during my brief tenure in the military, and I was awarded a few medals for my efforts. I keep the official narrative that is given with each medal on my desk. These awards hold more significance to me than any recognition I have received in the civilian world.

Service members who decide to make the military their career will have many opportunities to build expertise in a variety of professional and personal areas. Also, the longer someone is in the military and continues to prove themselves through leadership, commitment, and accomplishments, the more likely they are to be asked to lead troops, and they will be recognized for their efforts through promotions, medals, and awards.

"Our debt to the heroic son and valiant women in the service of our country can never be repaid. They have earned our

undying gratitude. America will never forget their sacrifices." - Harry Truman

Chapter 12. Cons of Joining

Any decision you make in life will have pros and cons. I have talked a lot about the benefits of joining the military and why it was one of the best decisions I have made in my life. However, I would be remiss if I did not discuss some of the potential cons of joining the military.

The United States military is the most disciplined work environment there is. As an airman, I had to keep my hair cut to a certain length, maintain certain physical standards, undergo random drug tests, and always be on time for work. In many ways, I became the property of the US government.

The United States military is built on a hierarchy, with commissioned officers on the top and enlisted soldiers below them. It does not matter if you are older than someone; if they have a higher rank, you need to listen to their instructions. This is usually not a big issue; however, rank has its privileges. When you first join, you will be lowest person on the totem pole, so you will be taking orders far more often than giving them. However, as your career advances, you will start being the one giving the instructions.

When you join the military, you make a legal commitment with the government. You sign a contract when you join and become legally responsible for fulfilling the terms of that contract. The consequences for deserting or quitting is severe and will likely end in a dishonorable discharge, forfeiture of pay, and possible confinement. In the civilian world, a person will typically give an employer two weeks' notice if they decide to quit. This is not an option in the military.

Depending on your occupation and how long you serve in the military, you may be deployed to a conflict. As I mentioned earlier, I deployed to a couple conflicts during my short military commitment. I have also known people who served for ten or fifteen years without ever being deployed.

When I was deployed, I was twenty-one years old and single. Deployments can be very hard for service members that are married and/or have children. Parents will miss their children's activities, and the time away can put pressure on the spouse who is not deployed.

You will likely not be stationed near the place you grew up. Therefore, separation from family could be challenging for you. At first, I was homesick and missed my being with friends and family. However, I gradually became more independent and mature and made new friends.

In the civilian world, you normally choose your work schedule. If you want to work from eight to five every day, you will likely not accept a job where you are expected to work nights and weekends. In the military, you do not get to choose the hours you work.

At my first duty station, I worked from approximately eight to five for one year. Then, I was promoted to a new position where I worked a week of day shifts (from seven to four), a week of mid shifts (from four to eleven), and a week of night shifts (from eleven to seven) and then had a week off. My body had a hard time adjusting to those different schedules. Luckily, I only had to do that for one year.

Transitioning back into the civilian world after serving in the military can be challenging. The military provides well-defined roles, missions, and a sense of purpose, all of which can be lacking or unclear in the civilian workplace.

Depending on your job duties and the areas of the world where you serve, you could experience depression or anxiety as a result of your experiences. Veterans Affairs has a variety of mental-health resources, information, and treatment options. There may also be a support group in your local area.

Still, for me, the benefits of serving my country far outweighed any cons.

"Face your challenges head-on rather than surrendering your dreams to fear." - Frank Sonnenberg

Chapter 13. Answer the Call

When I was nineteen years old, I was unsure of my future and purpose in life. I was fortunate to have a good friend serving in the military as well as a neighbor who was a military recruiter. Both gave me good insight on an option other than continuing my education at that point in my life.

Some people do not understand the military or may be opposed to you joining. When I told my mom, who administered the ASVAB test to high school students, that I was considering joining the military, she tried to talk me out of it. This is a common response for parents. They worry about their child going off to a conflict and not returning home.

Fortunately, the chances of being killed in a war today are much lower than in previous wars, such as World Wars I and II, the Korean War, and the Vietnam War.

To be clear, I don't want to minimize the risk of military personnel dying in combat or in training missions, because it does happen. Less than a year after I had completed my four-year military commitment and was attending college, I received word that one of the AC-130 aircraft I had deployed with had crashed off the Kenyan Coast. Eight of the fourteen people on board were killed. I knew every single one of them, and one was a good friend of mine. We would work out at the gym together and often hung out. He was ten years older than me, and I will never forget his wisdom and sense of humor.

When you make the commitment to join the military, there is always a chance that you will be deployed to a foreign conflict and be placed in some dangerous positions. Also, there are higher-risk positions in the military like explosive ordnance disposal technician, where you will detect, disarm, and dispose of explosive threats. Such positions face great risks even during training and peacetime exercises. However, it's important to keep in mind that there have been many more murders in the United States in the last decade than casualties of war.

The benefits you will receive from joining the military are limitless, and it's up to you on how you want to utilize them. You will gain significant knowledge from your superiors, which you can utilize whether you make the military your career or return to the civilian world. You will have opportunity to attend college, with the government paying part or all of the cost. You will have healthcare and dental benefits while you are serving and when your service is complete. You will make lifelong friends. You will learn discipline, leadership, and courage. You will be part of the minority of the population who was brave enough to take on the challenge and honor of serving your country. You will face adversity and stressful situations and learn how to adapt.

I highly recommend talking with your local recruiter as well as a MEPS career counselor to make sure you can find the military occupation that best fits your skill set; this will make your military experience more rewarding.

In high school, I never thought about or even considered joining the military. I planned to graduate from high school, enjoy the summer after, and then attend college, like many of my friends. I ended up doing that and was not happy or focused. I ended up being a teenager who wasn't sure what to do next. I could have continued in college; maybe I would have buckled down or maybe not. I could have started working full-time at some minimum-wage job. Instead, I chose to join the military, and it was the best decision I ever made. The military has rewarded me in so many ways. I strongly believe that I would not have finished college and been able to achieve success in the civilian world if I had not joined the military.

I strongly encourage you to visit a few recruiters and talk to any active-duty personnel or veterans you know so they can answer any questions you may have. I have also included my personal email address on the back cover of this book, and I would be glad to answer any questions you may still have after reading the book.

I served my country for only four years. I am not some long-tenured and highly decorated veteran and do not claim to be. I was fortunate enough to work alongside some very talented service members who ended up making the military their career, and they had a great deal of success in doing so. My purpose in writing this book is to help the young person who is lost and uncertain of their future, much like I was at nineteen. My answer was joining the military.

The military is actively seeking new recruits, as overall enlistment numbers are down across all branches. This results in a great opportunity for you, as there are sign-on bonuses for certain job categories, some changes in physical requirements, and many other changes in past requirements to get the enlistment numbers back up.

I wish you the best as you continue your research on joining the military, and I hope you answer the call to serve our great nation.

"It is the soldier, not the poet, who has given us freedom of speech." - Zell Miller

Glossary

The United States military is known for having its own alphabet as well as its own terminology or acronyms. I have included the military alphabet below as well as some of the more common military terms, which will assist you if you decide to join.

Military Alphabet

A -	Alpha	N -	November
B -	Bravo	O -	Oscar
C -	Charlie	P -	Papa
D -	Delta	Q -	Quebec
E -	Echo	R -	Romeo
F -	Foxtrot	S -	Sierra
G -	Golf	T -	Tango
H -	Hotel	U -	Uniform
I -	India	V -	Victor
J -	Juliet	W-	Whiskey
K -	Kilo	X -	X-ray
L -	Lima	Y -	Yankee
M -	Mike	Z -	Zulu

ABU–Airman Battle Uniform

ACU–Army Combat Uniform

AFSC–Air Force Specialty Code

AOR–Area of Responsibility

APO–Army Post Office (overseas address)

AWOL–Absent Without Leave (Army and Air Force)

Base–Air Force or Navy Installation

Battle Rattle–Body armor/battle gear

Boots on the ground–Deployed personnel landing in theater

BX–Base Exchange

CO–Commanding Officer

DADT–"Don't Ask, Don't Tell"

DD214–Certificate of release or discharge from active-duty service

DFAC–Dining facility/mess hall

Down range–Deployed

EOD–Explosive Ordinance Disposal

FOB–Forward Operating Base; Forward Operations Base

Garrison–A body of troops; the place where such troops are stationed; any military post, especially a permanent one

GWOT–Global War on Terrorism

HBCT–Heavy Brigade Combat Team

IBCT–Infantry Brigade Combat Team

IED/VBED–Improvised Explosive Device/Vehicle-Borne Explosive Device

RR–Individual Ready Reserve

JAG–Judge Advocate General (military lawyers)

Kevlar–Typically the helmet made of the material Kevlar

Leave–Off duty (usually vacation)

MEDEVAC–Medical Evacuation

MEU–Marine Expeditionary Unit

MOB/DEMOB–Mobilization/Demobilization

MOB–Main Operating Base

MOPP–Mission Oriented Protective Postures

MOS–Military Occupational Specialty

MP–Military Police (Air Force is SF –Security Forces)

MRAP–Mine-Resistant Ambush

MRE–Meal, Ready to Eat

NBC–Nuclear, Biological, and Chemical

NCO–Non-Commissioned Officer

NEC–Naval Enlisted Classification

NJP–Non-Judicial Punishment

PCS–Permanent Change of Station

Sick Call–Time allotted to see medical personnel

SNCO–Senior Non-Commissioned Officer

TAD–Temporary Area of Duty

TDY–Temporary Duty

Theater–The geographical area for which a commander of a geographic combatant command has been assigned responsibility

UA–Unauthorized Absence

UCMJ–Uniform Code of Military Justice (the foundation of military law

UXO–Unexploded Ordinance

XO–Executive Officer

There are other military terms as well as branch-specific terms. These are just the most common terms.

"Never regard study as a duty, but as the enviable opportunity to learn." - Albert Einstein

Steven J. Crane grew up in Iowa. After spending a year in college, he realized he needed a change. He joined the United States Air Force as an intelligence analyst, ultimately deploying to a couple conflicts. Joining the military was the best decision he ever made. He gained self-confidence and courage and developed leadership and time-management skills on his journey. After the military, he finished college and has spent the past twenty-five years as a bank executive.

Crane can be reached at sjcranenline@gmail.com.